16.00

DIVING AND SNORKELING GUIDE TO 🐚🐚🐚🐚🐚🐚🐚🐚🐚🐚

The Great Lakes

Lakes Superior, Michigan, Huron, Erie, and Ontario

Kathy Johnson and Greg Lashbrook

Pisces Books
A Division of Gulf Publishing Company
Houston, Texas

Acknowledgments

We wish to thank the following individuals for their assistance in preparing this guide: Jim Berry, Berry Scuba; Mike and Linda Kohut; Peter Lindquist; Bill and Ruthann Beck; Larry McElroy; Russ and Sue MacNeal; Jay Harris; Jeff Fox; Gerry Guyer; Bill Gardner; Rod Althaus; Alan Liles; and Wayne Brusate.

Publisher's note: At the time of publication of this book, all the information was determined to be as accurate as possible. However, when you use this guide, new construction may have changed land reference points, weather may have altered underwater configurations, and some businesses may no longer be in operation. Your assistance in keeping future editions up-to-date will be greatly appreciated.

Also, please pay particular attention to the diver rating system in this book. Know your limits!

Library of Congress Cataloging-in-Publication Data

Johnson, Kathy, 1965-
  Diving and snorkeling guide to the Great Lakes: Lake Superior, Lake Michigan, Lake Huron, Lake Erie, Lake Ontario / Kathy Johnson and Greg Lashbrook.
      p.   cm.
  Includes index.
  ISBN 1-55992-046-7
  1. Skin diving—Great Lakes—Guide-books. 2. Scuba diving—Great Lakes—Guide-books. 3. Great Lakes Region—Description and travel—Guide-books. I. Lashbrook, Greg. II. Title.
GV840.S78J635   1990
797.2'3—dc20   90-20474
                                                      CIP

Printed in Hong Kong

10 9 8 7 6 5 4 3 2 1

Table of Contents

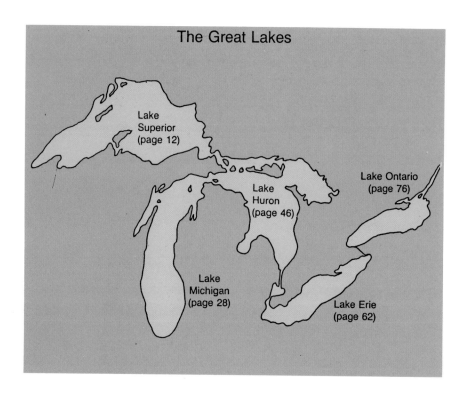

The Great Lakes

Lake Superior
(page 12)

Lake Huron
(page 46)

Lake Ontario
(page 76)

Lake Michigan
(page 28)

Lake Erie
(page 62)

Divers ready their gear aboard the charter boat, Straits Diver, *as they head toward the dive site.*

How To Use This Guide

This underwater guidebook does not, by any means, include all of the possible dive sites in the Great Lakes. To try to list every site in one book would be nearly impossible because the Great Lakes consist of over 52,000 square miles and together hold anywhere from 3,000 to 10,000 shipwrecks. Instead, this guide will direct divers to some of the best areas for diving in each of the five lakes. A few special sites have been selected for each area. A short history is included with each site, as well as information about what the diver can expect to see on bottom. Depth, water conditions, and skill level recommendations are also included. The maps of each lake provide a more extensive list of dive sites. They are intended to give divers a more complete idea of what each lake has to offer. A list of dive shops and charter services has been provided for each lake. These shops will be happy to provide divers with information on additional sites in their area.

Rating System for Divers and Dives

This guide's suggestions for the minimum level of experience should be taken in a conservative sense. Each diver should know his or her level of experience and limitations. For the purposes of this book, a *novice diver* is someone in good physical condition who has recently been certified, or a *certified diver* who has not dove in the past twelve months or is unfamiliar with the waters. An *intermediate diver* is someone in good physical condition who has been diving actively for at least one year following a certification course and has been diving recently in similar waters. An *advanced diver* is someone in excellent physical condition who has achieved an advanced level of diving certification and regularly dives in similar waters. Each diver, of course, must determine if he/she meets these requirements. When unsure of a dive, it is usually best to dive with someone more experienced or stay with the divemaster when on a professional charter. Always remember that water conditions can change at any time, even during a dive.

1

Overview of the Great Lakes

The divers grasp the down line and draw themselves into the silent depths. As they descend, they enter into a liquid time machine. Transported through the ages, they arrive on the foredeck of a nineteenth-century wooden schooner. Superbly preserved, it rests upright in its watery grave. The divers pause only for a moment. Time in this world is limited. They look around half expecting to see ancient sailors scurrying along the deck. The divers turn and quickly head for the bow. Easing themselves over the railing, they glide over the massive anchors that were never let out. Then scanning the area, they see it. A face of solid oak intricately carved into the bow. It gazes out majestically, eternally, ever ready to guide the ship in her travels. The divers gently run their fingers over the face, awed by its silent beauty and power. Their time is up too soon. They must return to their dive boat. At the mooring line they begin their ascent to the commonplace world above water. The ship gradually disappears into the darkness beneath them. Each diver is filled with his/her own vision of sailing ships and rugged sailors. Peering downward, the vision remains, but the ship is gone.

The Inland Seas

The Great Lakes are as unique as the manmade pyramids of Egypt, as fierce as the mighty oceans, and as clear as the tears of a child. These lakes are the largest concentration of freshwater on the planet. They hold over 65 trillion gallons of water, enough to cover all of the continental United States to a depth of ten feet. Together they have more shoreline than the entire Atlantic coast of the United States. A journey from Duluth in Lake Superior to the Atlantic Ocean covers almost 2,400 miles.

These inland seas are respected for their power and fury. At the time of their creation, thousands of years ago by the glaciers, enormous mountains of ice, gravel, and sand 200 feet high and 300 miles wide gouged deep trenches in the earth's crust. Later, mastodons and mammoths

2

A fall storm lashes out above the Fort Gratiot lighthouse at the south end of Lake Huron.

roamed the area. Still later, the Indians who lived along these shores believed the underwater world was ruled by evil spirits. The first Europeans learned of the lakes' fury when their first sailing ship, the *Griffon,* disappeared on its maiden voyage. More recently, lake freighters and their crews learned to respect these powerful waters. Man may have tamed the land, but no one has been able to conquer these mighty seas. They reign supreme.

Big Ships

By the late 1700s, hundreds of wooden schooners plied the hazardous waterways of the Great Lakes daily. They carried shiploads of supplies west from New England and returned with furs and raw materials for the East.

Technology advanced quickly during this period. By the early 1800s, wooden steamships appeared, followed in the 1880s by the first steel-hulled steamers. The older wooden steamers were pushed to their limits, and once-elegant schooners were converted to barges.

A "salty," shown here passing under the Blue Water bridge, works its way down through the lakes.

This was a dangerous time for ships on the Great Lakes. Navigational instruments were limited to a compass and a good captain. Ships were lost daily to weather, poor navigational skills, and carelessness. The United States' commissioner of navigation reported that in just a twenty-year period, between 1878-1898, 5,999 vessels were wrecked on the lakes. Of these, 1,093 were a total loss.

By the early 1900s, wooden ships were obsolete. The new era of steel had arrived. Shipping of grains, iron ore, copper, and lumber became an established and prosperous industry. The improvement of navigational instruments and the development of Coast Guard rescue stations greatly reduced the number of ships and lives lost each year.

However, these inland seas proved their ferocity in the storm of 1913. This three-day gale is considered the worst in the recorded history of the lakes. Blowing from November 9 through November 13, it destroyed 19 ships, stranded 19 more, and killed approximately 224 people.

There were two or three major shipping disasters during the 1950s and '60s. However, none received much attention outside of the Great Lakes shipping industry. In fact, it wasn't until 1975, when Lake Superior erupted in a raging fury, that the lakes gained the attention of the world. During this November storm, the 729-foot *Edmund Fitzgerald* went down, taking all of her crew with her. This disaster would most likely have been of interest only to the Great Lakes area had it not been for a song written by Gordon Lightfoot. His words immortalized the *Fitzgerald* and helped remind the world of the unconquerable strength of the Great Lakes:

Lake Huron rolls, Superior sings
In the rooms of her icewater mansions
Old Michigan steams like a young man's dream
Her islands and bays are for sportsmen
And further below Lake Ontario
Takes in what Lake Erie can send her
And the iron boats go as the mariners all know
With the gales of November remembered.

— *Wreck of the Edmund Fitzgerald* by Gordon Lightfoot
© 1976 Moose Music Inc. Used with permission.

The Great Lakes Today

The incredible maritime history of the Great Lakes offers a unique opportunity to divers. Nowhere else on earth can one find such an abundant selection of pristine wrecks. The Great Lakes, with their cool, clear waters, hold anywhere from 3,000 to 10,000 wrecks. Divers can swim along the deck of a seventeenth-century schooner, or peer through the pilot house window of a modern-day freighter.

The Great Lakes will continue to hold and preserve our past for generations to come. With the aid of divers and the establishment of underwater preserves, these links to our country's past will remain intact and undisturbed for everyone to enjoy. The Great Lakes are a sight and experience no diver should miss.

2

Diving the Great Lakes

Preserves

Underwater preserves are relatively new in the Great Lakes. The first one was established in 1981, in the Thunder Bay area of Lake Huron. Since then six others have been established, including: Whitefish Point in Lake Superior, the Straits of Mackinaw, Manitou Passage in Lake Michigan, the Thumb area in Lake Huron, Sanilac Shores in Lake Huron, and Alger in Superior. A new preserve is being formed off of Rogers City, Michigan, in Lake Huron.

The purpose of preserves is simply to protect and maintain the bottomlands of the Great Lakes. The location of each preserve is carefully researched and analyzed before it is approved. Historical significance, threatened resources, and natural or cultural features are a few of the requirements for an underwater preserve.

The state of Michigan is a leader in establishing underwater preserves, mainly owing to the support and interest of sport divers, charter boat operators, local citizens, and civil authorities. However, the preserves are only as successful as the vigilance of the divers who visit them. Divers are

---

Preserves and Underwater Parks

Preserves are not the same as underwater parks. Although both exist for identical reasons, they are different in several major ways. Underwater parks offer service facilities with informative, educational programs. Two underwater parks have been created in the Great Lakes: Isle Royale in Lake Superior and Tobermory in Lake Huron. Preserves, on the other hand, offer no services. They are simply recognized areas of interest that do not provide any specific recreational or educational facilities.

Fewer than ten located wrecks in the Great Lakes display a figurehead.

on the honor system. Please don't remove any artifacts that belong to or have come from a wreck or historical site. Let future divers enjoy the beauty and history of the Great Lakes.

Weather Patterns

Summer: Diving in the Great Lakes reaches its peak in July, August, and September. Earlier in the season, water temperatures are still quite cool. By mid-summer, though, water in the lower lakes reaches the upper 60s while the upper lakes reach into the upper 50s. The Great Lakes can provide beautiful diving weather. Days are in the 70s and 80s, with comfortable nights in the 60s to 70s.

Fall diving in the lakes can also be very enjoyable. The lower lakes often stay warm late into the fall and the changing fall colors offer a spectacular backdrop for boating or diving. However, fall storms are unpredictable, and most dive charters stop running in early October.

Winter: Many people assume diving in the Great Lakes ends with the first freeze. This is untrue. Ice diving has become more and more popular

Presque Isle lighthouse is the tallest lighthouse on the Great Lakes. Mariners still rely on lighthouses for pinpointing their location and for weather forecasts.

with the advent of high-performance dry suits. It offers the adventurous diver a unique opportunity to experience the mystery and beauty of a frozen underwater world. As with other specialties, ice diving requires special certification and gear. Many dive shops throughout the Great Lakes region offer certification classes.

Water Conditions

Water conditions can vary significantly among the five Great Lakes. This book explains some of the basic conditions with which divers should be familiar.

Currents: Because all water in the Great Lakes is in motion, divers commonly encounter currents. If you are caught unexpectedly in a strong current while diving from a boat, inflate your buoyancy compensator, and upon surfacing signal the boat, and gently kick towards the boat. When diving from shore, you should check conditions before entering the water. If the current seems to be more than your experience permits, you should either terminate the dive or change locations.

Visibility: Water clarity, or visibility, is based on the distance a diver can see objects clearly underwater. For example, if water visibility is ten feet, then the diver can clearly see objects ten feet away. Objects any further will appear hazy or nonexistent. The visibility of any area can change daily with weather conditions. Divers should always check visibility before a dive and be alert to visibility changes during a dive. If the clarity decreases significantly while underwater, the diver should be aware that surface conditions may also be changing.

Thermocline: Thermoclines are formed when warm surface waters meet colder, deeper waters. The exact depth where this happens varies from site to site, even from day to day. Generally, thermoclines are reached at a depth of about 15 to 40 feet. Divers should know whether they will be diving in a thermocline. Surface temperatures can be in the high 60s; however, beneath the thermocline, temperatures could easily be in the 30s to 40s. In these conditions, a dry suit or a good cold-water wetsuit, including farmer johns, chicken vest, cold-water hood, and three-fingered mitts, is recommended.

Divers frequently encounter currents when diving in the Great Lakes, so plan accordingly.

Boat Diving

Charter boats are the most trouble-free way to enjoy Great Lakes diving. Charters can spare the diver the worries of weather, navigation, and site location. Organized charters can also cut down on travel time by quickly and easily locating the best dive sites.

There are two cardinal rules of boat diving. The first is *keep your equipment together*. This is especially important on crowded charter boats. Once you are out of the water, your mask, fins, and weight belt should be stowed away. Designate one area for all your equipment — and keep it there!

The second rule of boat diving is *know where the down line is* and know how to get back to it. Whether the boat is anchored or tied-off to a mooring, you should always know how to return to your boat. In poor visibility or on unfamiliar wrecks, never venture too far from the line. Remember to put safety first!

There are many full-service dive shops throughout the Great Lakes that will be happy to assist with charters and equipment rental and repair. Group rates are also available through several charters.

Although charters are convenient, some divers may wish to use their own boats. Remember to take extra precautions in unfamiliar waters. Charts, weather reports, and water conditions should be checked before heading out. All the underwater preserves have a standardized buoy system

Wreck Diving

The Great Lakes have the best wreck diving in the world. Nowhere else can the diver find such an intense concentration of sunken ships preserved so superbly. From seventeenth-century wooden schooners to nineteenth-century super freighters, the Great Lakes have them all. These inland seas hold thousands of sunken vessels in a watery time capsule.

But the shipwrecks of the Great Lakes offer divers more than a unique look at the history of maritime architecture. Their cargos of clothing, food, tools, and utensils provide divers with a slice of life of the "old" days. Only in the Great Lakes can you travel from century to century, experiencing a way of life as it once was.

Penetrating sunken shipwrecks can be very dangerous for the untrained diver. This exacting sport requires special certification and equipment similar to that used in ice and cave diving. Many of the full-service dive shops offer classes in wreck diving. Certification classes include several dives on some of the best wrecks in the Great Lakes. Divers planning a trip to the lakes should consider a wreck-diving course. These classes are an interesting and safe introduction to Great Lakes shipwrecks.

Diving Regulations

Flags: According to international law, all boats in open waters must fly an Alpha flag. The Alpha flag signals that the boat is under restricted maneuverability. This flag must be flown by all boats on the Great Lakes.

The *divers down* flag must be flown while divers and snorkelers are in the water. (The *divers down* flag must be at least 14 inches by 16 inches. It consists of a red background with a white diagonal stripe. The stripe must be at least 3½ inches wide.) State requirements for distance between divers and their flags vary. For Michigan, Ohio, New York, and Wisconsin the distance is 100 feet. For Minnesota and Illinois, the distance is only 50 feet. The distance boats must maintain from a *divers down* flag varies from 100 to 200 feet. When operating your own boat, it's best to play it safe by maintaining the maximum distance required.

"Divers-Down" Flag

Alpha Flag International signal meaning "I have a diver down; keep clear and at a slow speed."

Fishing: Spearfishing is not allowed for sport fish in any state around the Great Lakes. In most states besides Michigan, divers are allowed to take a certain number of rough fish at certain times of the year. Check local regulations *before* entering the water with a speargun. In many states, it is illegal to even have a speargun in the water out of season. Spearfishermen must have a current state fishing license.

11

3

Lake Superior

The national weather bureau had forecast a strong weather system approaching from the northeast. But Captain McSorley, master of the *Edmund Fitzgerald*, wasn't too concerned. The *Fitzgerald* was a strong ship, a 729-foot ultra-modern freighter that was more than capable of handling a bit of rough weather. Captain McSorley was also well seasoned. He had been working the Great Lakes for forty-four years, and during that time he had been through several "blows." His experiences taught him great respect for these inland seas. After considering the weather reports, he steered a course for the north shore of Superior. If this storm took a turn for the worse, the north shore could offer protection.

Passing Two Harbors, the *Fitzgerald* met up with the *Arthur M. Anderson,* which was also headed for the Soo. The two captains maintained radio contact, discussed the weather reports, and agreed to continue hugging the north shore. By 1 a.m. the winds were gusting to 60 miles per hour and ten-foot waves pounded both ships. However, they were still making good progress.

Around 2 a.m., the weather bureau posted an update. Gale warnings were changed to storm warnings, which is the severest possible forecast. The bureau also reported that the winds would be changing to northwest as the storm crossed Lake Superior.

By 10 a.m. the morning of November 10, the *Fitzgerald* and the *Anderson* reached the eastern end of Lake Superior. From there they headed south towards Whitefish Bay. Near Caribou Island, the ships were about 15 miles apart. The winds were in excess of 40 knots, creating 15–20-foot waves. Both ships struggled as the seas crashed into their sterns, threatening to broach them.

The *Fitzgerald* was having problems. Her primary radar wasn't functioning, leaving her with only a small secondary radar for guidance. At this point, the *Fitzgerald* probably passed too close to the shoal just off Caribou Island. The fully-loaded freighter drew almost 30 feet, and the shoal was only 36 feet deep. In the wild, plunging seas the *Fitzgerald* most likely bottomed on the reef, damaging her hull.

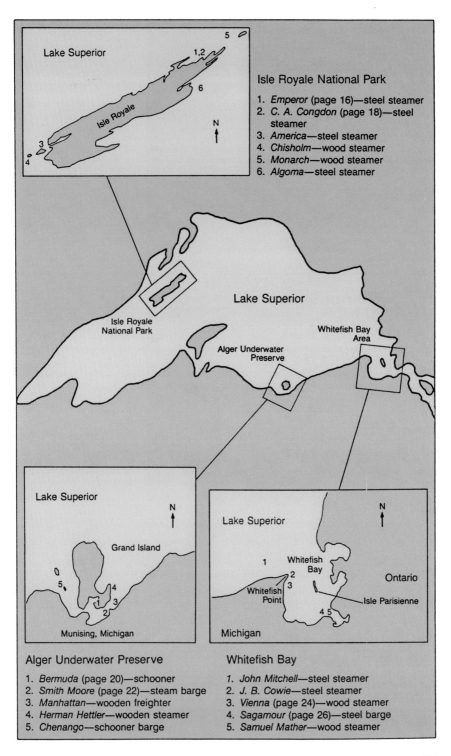

Lake Superior

Isle Royale National Park

1. *Emperor* (page 16)—steel steamer
2. *C. A. Congdon* (page 18)—steel steamer
3. *America*—steel steamer
4. *Chisholm*—wood steamer
5. *Monarch*—wood steamer
6. *Algoma*—steel steamer

Isle Royale

N

Lake Superior

Isle Royale
National Park

Whitefish Bay
Area

Alger Underwater
Preserve

Lake Superior

N

Grand Island

Munising, Michigan

Lake Superior

N

Whitefish
Bay

Ontario

Whitefish
Point

Isle Parisienne

Michigan

Alger Underwater Preserve

1. *Bermuda* (page 20)—schooner
2. *Smith Moore* (page 22)—steam barge
3. *Manhattan*—wooden freighter
4. *Herman Hettler*—wooden steamer
5. *Chenango*—schooner barge

Whitefish Bay

1. *John Mitchell*—steel steamer
2. *J. B. Cowie*—steel steamer
3. *Vienna* (page 24)—wood steamer
4. *Sagamour* (page 26)—steel barge
5. *Samuel Mather*—wood steamer

The colorful sandstone
cliffs of Lake Superior's
south shore have inspired
poems, legends, and
novels.

As the *Fitzgerald* and the *Anderson* cleared Caribou Island, the captains again discussed conditions. Captain McSorley realized he had serious problems. He reported that two of his pumps were running and the ship was listing slightly. He had also lost his secondary radar and was now left with only a compass for navigation. McSorley made the critical decision to slow down to wait for the slower *Anderson,* and this put the *Fitzgerald* in a dangerous position. With the seas constantly trying to turn the ship, speed was essential. However, Captain McSorley was willing to trade seaworthiness for help if it became necessary.

By 6 p.m., the *Fitzgerald* was just 27 miles out of Whitefish Bay. But the storm had reached its peak. Winds were in excess of 90 miles per hour and the seas had reached 30 feet. Blankets of ice covered the ships and snow showers dropped visibility to a few feet. The first mate aboard the *Anderson* kept a close watch on the *Fitzgerald* with his radar.

Just after 7 p.m., the two ships entered a "white out." Blizzard conditions completely blocked the *Anderson*'s radar. For a brief 15 minutes, the ships were out of contact. When the snow lifted, the *Fitzgerald* was gone.

No survivors were ever found from the *Fitzgerald*. It is presumed that the ship was overcome by two waves of tremendous size. Slow to recover because of the water in her holds, the *Fitzgerald* nose-dived to the bottom of Lake Superior. Her battered hull was identified weeks later by side scan sonar in approximately 530 feet of water.

> The legend lives on from the Chippewa on down
> Of the big lake they call Gitche Gumme
> Superior they said never gives up her dead
> When the gales of November come early.

— From *Wreck of the Edmund Fitzgerald*

Lake Superior is the largest body of freshwater in the world and one of the deepest with a maximum depth of over 1,300 feet. Superior has the finest wreck diving in the world. Visibility averages between 30 and 40 feet throughout the summer, and over 50 feet is not uncommon. Its cold waters, which only reach the upper 30s below the thermocline, have kept Superior's shipwrecks in near perfect condition. Divers interested in the ultimate in wreck diving should visit Lake Superior.

Isle Royale, which lies about 10 miles off the north shore, is the largest island in Lake Superior. Over 20 miles long and 10 miles wide, it reigns over the western end of the lake. This island and the surrounding bottomlands have been part of Michigan's park system for over twenty years. The park headquarters offers information on dive sites, maps showing the location of wrecks, and camp site availability. There are also several privately owned dive charters that offer live-aboard services for divers interested in a truly relaxed vacation.

Three hundred miles to the southeast lies Alger Underwater Preserve. The preserve is just offshore of Munising on Lake Superior's south shore. Throughout the 1800s, Munising was a favorite harbor for ships traversing the lakes. The harbor, protected by Grand Island, which runs parallel to the shore, guarantees protection to any ship that could make it inside. Many didn't and now rest in peace on the lake's bottom.

Whitefish Bay in Superior's eastern corner is also an underwater preserve. This area is one of the most treacherous stretches in Lake Superior. For divers, it provides some of the best wreck diving in North America. The Great Lakes' Shipwreck Historical Museum is located on the tip of Whitefish Point. This museum offers audio and visual presentations on the history of shipping and diving in the Great Lakes. There are also several displays including artifacts from wrecks in the Whitefish area.

Emperor

Typical Depth :	25-60 feet (bow)
Typical Current :	Slight
Expertise Required :	Intermediate
Access :	Boat, Isle Royale National Park

A 525-foot steel-bulk carrier, the *Emperor* was the pride of the Canadian Steamships Line. At the time of her launching, she was the largest vessel ever built in Canada and the first of the 10,000 tonners to run the lakes. She was built in 1911 in Collingwood, Ontario, and for thirty-six years, prosperously worked the lakes — until the night of June 4, 1947.

The lighthouse at Blake Point on Isle Royale was improved after the *Chester A. Congdon* was stranded in 1918. A red light warned vessels approaching from the wrong direction. However, on the night of June 4, 1947, the captain and lookout on duty in the pilot house of the *Emperor* couldn't see the light. A storm was blowing and visibility was severely limited. Without warning, the *Emperor*'s bow ran hard aground on the reef. Within minutes, the ship went down, taking 12 of her crew with her. Today the bow lies in 25 to 60 feet of water.

The air vent on the stern of the Emperor *is large enough for this diver to fit inside.*

The Emperor's *starboard anchor is still housed and can still be seen resting against the ship's hull.*

Like many shallower wrecks, the *Emperor* has been severely damaged by ice over the years. Her pilot house is gone and much of the superstructure is dented and bent. Divers can see where the ship broke near the No. 4 cargo hold. The bow and stern are still connected; however, they are considered separate dives.

Both anchors can be seen on the bow. The starboard is still housed against the hull. The port is strung out and lies in the sand about 20 feet away. Looking under the forward decking, divers see hundreds of feet of anchor chain tumbled together like giant piles of spaghetti.

Much of the foredeck equipment is still in place — winches, windlass, and cleats. This is a good wreck for divers new to the area because it lies in shallow water and has outstanding visibility.

The stern section is much more intact because ice cannot damage it at 100 to 170 feet. However, this depth is beyond the limits of most sport divers, and only those certified as deep divers should make this dive. For those that do, a remarkably intact wreck is there to explore. Bunk beds are still in place in the cabins and the spare propeller blades rest on the aft deck.

Congdon Bow

Typical Depth :	70-110 feet
Typical Current :	Slight
Expertise Required :	Advanced/intermediate
Access :	Boat, Isle Royale National Park

Canoe Rocks is a shallow reef just off the north end of Isle Royale. The reef received its name from an outcropping of rocks that protrude several feet from the water and slightly resemble a canoe. Well off the normal steamer route, they posed little danger until the night of November 7, 1918. Lake Superior was in one of her typical foul November moods. The waves were building, visibility was limited, and the *Chester A. Congdon* was off course. Before long, the 532-foot steel-bulk freighter ran up on the jagged, shallow reef. The crew was saved, but the big ship broke into pieces before the storm was over. She became the first million-dollar loss on Lake Superior.

Even at a depth of 70 feet, Lake Superior is still bright and clear. Shown here is the pilot house of the Congdon.

This sign is bolted above one of the Congdon's doorways. Although it was meant for the ship's sailors, it carries an eerie message to divers in 110 feet of water.

The bow section is completely intact in 70 to 110 feet of water. It lies at a sharp 45° angle with the pilot-house windows looking up towards the surface. This is a wonderful dive for those not accustomed to deeper water. The mooring line is tied off on the tip of the bow in approximately 70 feet of water. The pilot house is open and easily accessible, the deck is uncluttered, and several staircases can be easily explored. By following the guidewires that run from the bow to the tip of the mast, divers can look back to see the complete bow section.

Grenada — Dreadnaught — Bermuda

Typical Depth :   12-30 feet
Typical Current :   None
Expertise Required :   Novice
Access :   Boat, Alger Underwater Preserve

One of the most controversial wrecks of Lake Superior is the schooner that lies in Murray's Bay off Munising. For years it was locally known as the *Grenada*. Later, researchers claimed it was actually the wreck of the *Dreadnaught*. Now, however, several well-known historians call it the wreck of the *Bermuda*. Unfortunately, no one has been able to find the serial numbers that were carved in the hull of all wooden ships. These numbers would forever end the controversy over the identity of the wreck.

Assuming that this wreck is the *Bermuda*, we know that she was used as a tow barge before sinking. In the late 1800s, it was common practice to leave barges in protected bays for the winter. It was also common for

This diver is peering out from a cargo hold on the Bermuda's *stern deck.*

Here, a diver poses on the bow railing of the Bermuda, *an eighteenth-century wooden schooner.*

the seams of wooden ships to leak. In fact, most ships were overhauled each spring including having all their seams recaulked. Unfortunately, the owner of the *Bermuda* returned to Murray's Bay too late. The once-proud ship had filled with water and settled to the bottom. She now lies in an upright position.

When the *Bermuda* was converted to a barge, most of her sail rigging was removed. Over the years, vandals have taken the rest. And yet, she is still a fabulous wreck.

In just 12 to 30 feet of water, this is a fantastic wreck for divers and snorkelers. The bay waters are calm, crystal clear and warm compared to Lake Superior standards. A large school of bass and numerous suckers congregate on the stern deck, creating a near-tropical atmosphere.

21

Smith Moore

Typical Depth :	80-105 feet
Typical Current :	Variable: slight to moderate
Expertise Required :	Advanced
Access :	Boat, Alger Underwater Preserve

The *Smith Moore* was a three-decked wooden steam barge used for bulk cargos. She was one of the transitional ships that came between the wind-powered schooners and the steam-powered freighters. Built in 1880, the *Smith Moore* was rigged with three masts, but ran on coal. The masts could be used for auxiliary power if necessary and also provided stability while underway.

On the night of July 13, 1889, a thick fog covered Lake Superior. The *Moore* was downbound with a load of iron ore. The *James Pickands*, however, was on an upbound course. During the night, the two ships collided leaving the *Moore* mortally wounded. The *Pickands* was unharmed and continued on her course. The captain of the *Pickands* later claimed he never heard the *Moore*'s distress signals.

A staircase leads below deck on the Smith Moore. *(Photo courtesy of the Alger Underwater Preserve.)*

Ropes have been used to tie together scattered pieces of wreckage in the Alger Preserve. The ropes help divers make their way from piece to piece.

Left on her own, the *Moore* drifted aimlessly until morning. When the fog lifted, the *M.M. Drake* spotted the *Smith Moore* and came to her aid. The *Drake* took the *Moore*'s crew on board and began towing the wounded ship towards Munising. The fate of the *Moore* was already sealed, however. She continued to take on water until the drag finally broke the tow line. She sank immediately in 105 feet of water, just off Munising in the east channel.

However, Lake Superior was not finished with the *Smith Moore*. Over the last few years, several storms have hit the Munising area. Sand washed up from a nearby sandbar slowly covered the wreck, stern first. The huge ship's propellers that were once a favorite of local divers are now completely buried under 20 feet of sand.

In the summer of 1989, divers working with the approval of the Alger Underwater Preserve removed sand from the stern of the ship. Diving in shifts for days, they managed to uncover the stern decking (the propellers remain covered). Today, the ship rests peacefully, with the sand held at bay. We hope Superior will allow her to remain for our enjoyment.

Vienna

Typical Depth :	100-150 feet
Typical Current :	None
Expertise Required :	Advanced
Access :	Boat, Whitefish Bay

September 16, 1892 was a bright, sunny day. The wooden steamer *Vienna* was downbound with the barge *Mattie C. Beel* in tow. The *Vienna*'s sister ship, the *Nipagone*, was upbound with two barges of her own in tow. As was customary, the two steamers drew close to exchange greetings. Sailors waved and called out to friends they hadn't seen in many months. The two ships' captains saluted, then ordered their ships back on course. However, quite unexpectedly, the *Nipagone* veered directly towards the *Vienna*. Before the *Vienna*'s crew could react, she was hit broadside.

It was immediately obvious that the *Vienna* was badly hurt. Dropping their tow barges, the steamers once again came together. All of the *Vienna*'s crew was transferred to the *Nipagone*. With everyone safely aboard, the *Nipagone* began towing the *Vienna* into shore. She almost made it to safety, but just half a mile from shore, the *Vienna* sank to her grave.

The *Vienna* is one of the more popular dives in Whitefish Bay. Because she lies close to shore and is inside Whitefish point, she is sheltered from the weather. She sits upright on the bottom with most of her hull intact. The stern railings are still standing, but her superstructure has been washed away. Both the boilers and engine are clearly visible and easy to explore. The rudder and prop are still on the stern; however, her name has faded and now requires a little imagination to see. Towards the bow, divers can find one of her lifeboats still on the deck.

This is a deep dive, but has much to offer the advanced diver. The outstanding visibility in the area (average of 40 feet) provides adequate light, even at this depth, but a dive light is recommended for seeing more clearly into the wreck.

This diver is small enough to peek out of a hole in the ship's decking.

Sagamore

Typical Depth :	45-65 feet
Typical Current :	None
Expertise Required :	Novice/intermediate
Access :	Boat, Whitefish Bay

The whaleback or "pigboat" was designed to provide minimal resistance to wind and waves and yet be fast and seaworthy. Its rounded sides and stub nose gave it the appearance of a floating hot dog. However, as strange as it looked, it was the leading carrier of iron ore in the early 1900s.

The *Sagamore* was a whaleback barge. She was built in 1892 in Wisconsin and was towed by the *Pathfinder*, also a whaleback. The two ships were anchored on July 29, 1901 at the southern end of Whitefish Bay. They were waiting out a thick fog that covered most of Lake Superior. Around 9 a.m., the steamer *North Queen* came flying out of the fog at

A lawyer fish, or burbot, is a stationary fish that looks somewhat like a catfish. They can usually be found lurking among a ship's decking or machinery.

A diver looks out through a doorway window. Lake Superior's clear, cool waters provide excellent photographic opportunities.

full speed. She rammed the *Sagamore*, fatally wounding her. The *Sagamore* sank quickly. Several of her crew managed to leap to safety aboard the *North Queen*; however, the captain and steward were lost.

The *Sagamore* gives divers the opportunity to examine a type of ship no longer seen on the lakes. It is made of riveted iron and is 308 feet long. She sits upright in 45 to 65 feet of water, which is quite shallow by Lake Superior standards. The fantastic visibility in the area, which averages 40 feet, offers almost unlimited investigation of the hull. The winch and anchor chains are still on the bow. Divers can peer into the anchor locker, but shouldn't try to penetrate. Divers can see the *Sagamore*'s mortal wound on the port side near the stern.

4

Lake Michigan

July 24, 1913 was a warm, sunny day and the employees of the Western Electric Company were in high spirits. Their families were being treated to a cruise aboard the *Eastland*. The day trip would take them from Chicago's harbor to Michigan City, Indiana. Everyone laughed and talked excitedly as they boarded the impressive ship. The *Eastland* was a 269-foot steel steamer, painted white and decorated with streamers for the day's excursion.

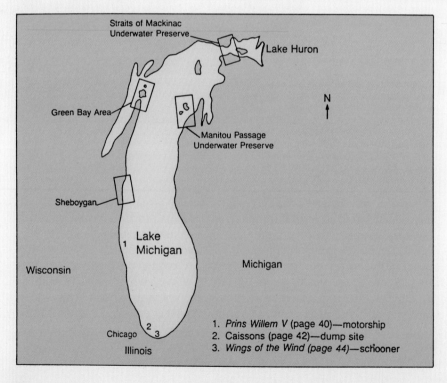

Straits of Mackinac
Underwater Preserve

1. *Northwest*—schooner
2. *Sandusky* (page 32)—brig schooner
3. *M. Stalker*—schooner
4. *Cedarville* (page 35)—propeller
5. *William H. Barnum*—propeller

Green Bay Area

1. *Hackett* (page 37)—steamer
2. *Gilmore*—schooner
3. *Pilot Island*—5 shipwrecks
4. *Riverside*—schooner
5. *Meridian*—schooner

Manitou Passage
Underwater Preserve

1. *Temperance*—schooner
2. *G. Knapp*—schooner
3. *Margaret Dall*—schooner
4. *Congress*—steamer
5. *The Three Brothers*—steamer

Note: Although these wrecks in the recently opened Manitou Passage Underwater Preserve are not described in this guide, charters are available in the area and divers are encouraged to explore these sites.

Sheboygan

1. *Selah. Chamberlain* (page 38)—steam barge
2. *Hattie Taylor*—schooner
3. *Advance*—schooner
4. *Atlanta*—steamer
5. *Niagara*—steamer

The Mackinaw Bridge has the longest span of any bridge on the Great Lakes. It connects Michigan's upper and lower peninsulas and separates Lake Michigan from Lake Huron.

The ship's band played a lively tune while the 2,500 excursionists crowded the decks waiting expectantly for the ship to shove off. Finally, the gangplank was pulled in and the stern line was cast off. But something was wrong. The ship had a severe list to port. A few of the partygoers noticed, but most continued celebrating, until the furniture started to slide. Suddenly children and adults were thrown against the railing or cabin walls as the ship began to roll on her side.

The *Eastland*'s chief engineer realized the problem. The ballast tanks beneath the ship had not been filled with water. Without this necessary stability, the ship could not remain upright. It would turn over, and there was nothing they could do to stop it. Women and children screamed as they were thrown into the frigid waters of Lake Michigan. Hundreds of passengers were trapped below deck and drowned as water poured into the ship's belly. Hundreds more scrambled onto the starboard side that remained 15 feet out of water.

People on the pier watched helplessly as body after body disappeared under the harbor's murky waters. A few passengers managed to grab floating pieces of furniture or boxes to help them remain afloat. But most perished. In less time than it took to load the boat, more than 800 people lost their lives. To this day, the capsizing of the *Eastland* remains the greatest single loss of life in the history of the Great Lakes.

Today, Chicago is the heart of Lake Michigan and the central distribution point of the United States. Millions of tons of cargo pass through its port each year. It has aptly been called the "Queen City of the West," "Gem of the Prairie," and "Queen of the Lakes." The tremendous boat traffic that this area sees every year provides Chicago with a large concentration of dive sites. Several full-service dive centers and charter services are available in the Chicago area.

Further up the west coast of Lake Michigan lie the cities of Milwaukee, Sheboygan, and Kewaunee. These areas abound with wrecks, from three-masted schooners to five-hundred-foot package freighters that in their day were the pride of the shipping industry.

Green Bay is the only natural harbor on the west coast of Lake Michigan. The narrow passageway into the bay was called "Death's Door" by early ship captains. Terrible fall storms that customarily hit this area have broken up most of the wrecks here. This is a good destination for less experienced divers. The average visibility is 20 to 30 feet and the average depth is 40 to 60 feet.

On the east coast of Lake Michigan is Manitou Underwater Preserve. This is the only underwater preserve in Lake Michigan. Manitou Preserve encompasses 282 square miles and has as many as 75 shipwrecks. However, dive charters in the area only visit about nine regularly.

Many of the cities on Michigan's west coast, such as Frankfort, Ludington, Muskegon, and Grand Haven, grew with the development of ferry boat traffic across Lake Michigan. The diving industry in these areas has grown also. These areas now offer dive charters, air fills and full-service dive shops.

Sandusky

Typical Depth :	65-90 feet
Typical Current :	Variable: slight to moderate
Expertise Required :	Intermediate
Access :	Boat, Straits of Mackinaw Underwater Preserve

The *Sandusky* is one of the truly majestic brig schooners of the 1800s. She is 110 feet long, has a square stern, double mast, and a hand-carved, scroll figurehead on her bow. She went down on September 18, 1856, just west of the Mackinaw Bridge. She took seven of her crew with her when she succumbed to a violent gale.

The *Sandusky* is one of the finest dives in the Great Lakes. She is perfectly intact and sits upright in 65 to 90 feet of water. Most of her original sailing rigging is still in place, although her masts are no longer standing. Fortunately, she has managed to evade severe looting over the years. The *Sandusky* is a superb example of a historic sailing vessel.

Her tiller and wheel lie broken on the sterndeck. However, the rest of the ship lies unbroken. The side railings are cluttered with deadeyes and mounts for missing belaying pins. The cargo holds draw the diver up to the windlass. Over the bow rails, anchors hang patiently, still waiting to be let out. But the crowning jewel of this wreck is the figurehead carved into the bow.

Less than ten located wrecks in the Great Lakes display a carved figurehead. With this in mind, it's hard to understand why any diver would attempt to remove one of these carvings from a wreck. Unfortunately, that is exactly what happened in 1988. Divers from the Straits Underwater Preserve discovered the figurehead loosened by vandals during the summer. Michigan's Department of Natural Resources removed the figurehead and placed it in a museum. It is currently being restored at the Maritime Museum in South Haven, Michigan.

During the winter of 1988-9, a project was begun to make and install an exact replica of the *Sandusky*'s figurehead. The project was a grand success and the figurehead has now been replaced. Special thanks goes to Tony Gramer and Franz Estereicher for their work on this project.

The new figurehead on the bow of the Sandusky *is an exact replica of the original.*▶

Cedarville

Typical Depth :	70-90 feet
Typical Current :	Variable: slight to moderate
Expertise Required :	Advanced
Access :	Boat, Straits of Mackinaw Underwater Preserve

The *Cedarville* rests just two and a half miles east of the Mackinaw Bridge. She was a 588-foot steel self-unloader built in 1927. During a light fog on the night of May 7, 1965, she was rammed by the Norwegian vessel *Toppalsfjord*. It was immediately obvious that the *Cedarville* had been mortally wounded. In a desperate attempt to save the ship and crew, the captain headed for shore. He planned to beach the *Cedarville* on the lower peninsula side of the straits. But before he could put her on the beach, she rolled to starboard and went down taking ten men with her. She now rests upside down in 70 to 90 feet of water.

The bow and stern are considered separate dives because of her 588-foot length. During the regular dive season, each end is marked with a mooring buoy. This wreck is disorientating for most divers. She lies upside down with a strange tilt to her port side. The angle this upside-down-listing creates can be confusing to divers, especially when visibility isn't ideal.

The Sandusky's *bow sprint is still covered with deadeyes and extends nearly ten feet out from the bow.* ◄

A diver playfully peers out of a porthole on the stern of the Cedarville.

The stern of the Cedarville has several rooms that divers can look into and see broken furniture and assorted debris.

The pilot house is mostly intact. The compass hangs from the ceiling (floor) and several control panels are still on the walls. Divers should be extremely cautious on this wreck. It is easy to become confused about which way is up. Only divers certified in wreck diving, using proper equipment and technique, should consider penetrating this wreck.

The *Cedarville*'s name can be clearly seen on the stern of the ship. The propeller is still in place, seemingly ready to continue the journey. Divers can also peer into the engine room and some of the crew's quarters without penetration. Floor tiles and pieces of broken furniture can be seen in most of the rooms. Again, only certified wreck divers should enter this or any wreck.

Hackett

Typical Depth :	15-20 feet
Typical Current :	Variable: slight to moderate
Expertise Required :	Novice
Access :	Boat

The *Hackett* was one of the original predecessors of today's bulk carriers. She was built in 1869 to carry grain and iron ore, which in the late 1800s, were quickly becoming profitable industries. The steambarges that proceeded the bulk carriers had schooner-like hulls and steam engines. Although they could carry some bulk cargoes, such as lumber, they didn't have adequate storage below decks for grains, coal, and ore. Also, their hatches were too narrow for the unloading equipment used at most large ports. Thus, ships like the *Hackett* were built to fit the needs of this new industry. The *Hackett* was constructed of wood and looked like a steambarge; however, her holds were large and evenly spaced and she was longer (211 feet).

Around 7 a.m. on November 12, 1905, the *Hackett* was east of Whaleback Shoal in Green Bay. She was upbound on Lake Michigan with a load of coal intended for Marinette, Michigan. Just after 7 a.m., a crew member reported to Captain McCallum that there was a fire in the crew's quarters. While the crew struggled to contain the blaze, Captain McCallum ordered the ship run aground on Whaleback Shoal. At one point, the crew thought they had beaten the flames, but a new outbreak started in the engine room. The flames ate their way through the engine room wall. Faced with this new inferno, the crew and captain wisely decided to abandon ship. Paddling off in two lifeboats, they watched as the ship exploded in flames. She burned to her water line and eventually settled to the bottom in 20 feet of water.

The *Hackett* is an excellent wreck for snorkelers and divers. Visibility averages 20 feet and water temperatures reach the high 60s during the summer. Parts of the ship's engines, the boiler, propeller, and pieces of the hull provide shelter for schools of perch, bass, lawyers, and carp.

Selah Chamberlain

Typical Depth :	60-80 feet
Typical Current :	Slight
Expertise Required :	Intermediate
Access :	Boat

The *Selah Chamberlain* was one of the original wooden single-screw steam barges. On the afternoon of October 13, 1886, she left Milwaukee heading for Escanaba for a load of iron ore. By 8:00 p.m. that same day, the *Chamberlain* was just off Sheboygan enveloped in a thick fog. Undaunted, she plowed on, sounding her whistle regularly. At 8:30 p.m. the captain heard the whistle of another steamer directly ahead. He blew one whistle, then put the *Chamberlain* hard aport. Unfortunately, he wasn't quick enough. The *Chamberlain* and the steam barge *John Pridgeon Jr.* collided with a splintering of wood and a grinding of metal.

The boilers that powered the Chamberlain *still contain pieces of coal.*

Bass are one of the most inquisitive of freshwater fishes. They seem to enjoy playing with visiting divers.

Almost immediately the two ships drifted apart. The *Pridgeon* disappeared into the fog and was not seen again by the surviving crew of the *Chamberlain*.

Captain Greeley of the *Chamberlain* ordered the lifeboats launched. Five of the crew perished when they foolishly jumped into a lifeboat before it reached the water. Their weight broke the davits, and they were thrown into the seas. The rest of the crew, including Captain Greeley, made a safe escape aboard the second lifeboat. The survivors watched through the dense fog as the *Chamberlain* sank into her watery grave. They then turned the lifeboat towards shore and headed in.

Today, the *Chamberlain* rests directly off Sheboygan Harbor. In 60 to 80 feet of water, with a large assortment of machinery still intact, it's an underwater photographer's dream. Looking into the gigantic boilers that fueled the ship, divers can still see large piles of unused coal. The warm water temperatures during the summer (mid 50s) and visibility averaging 15 to 20 feet make this a great dive.

Prins Willem V

Typical Depth :	90 feet
Typical Current :	Slight
Expertise Required :	Advanced
Access :	Boat

The *Prins Willem V* was a Dutch motorship (freighter) built in 1948. On October 14, 1954, she left Milwaukee with a load of heavy machinery and crates of musical instruments. Just outside Milwaukee's harbor she ran into the towline between a Sinclair tug and barge No. 12. The pressure on the towline drove the barge into the side of the *Willem*. Although she was fatally wounded, she drifted on the surface for several miles. All of her crew were able to safely abandon ship.

The Pirate's Cove Dive Shop has mounted this plaque on the Willem's *starboard rail. It tells the story of how and why the ship went down.*

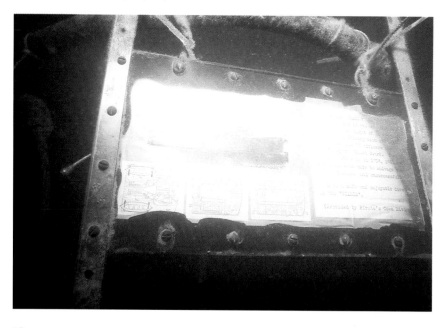

The Prins Willem*'s name can be easily read on the stern. She sailed under the Dutch flag.*

Salvage attempts were made after the *Willem*'s sinking. Most of the cargo was removed; however, the ship was left on bottom as a total loss. The hull is in perfect condition except for the area of the collision. The *Willem* sits upright with approximately a 60° list to starboard.

This wreck has much to offer the advanced diver. The rudder and name are visible on the stern although the propeller is missing. The ship has four cargo holds, two forward and two aft, with the superstructure in between. A diver can easily swim through the main wheel house and look into several cabin areas and the engine room.

The Caissons

Typical Depth :	40-45 feet
Typical Current :	Slight
Expertise Required :	Novice/intermediate
Access :	Boat

The year 1871 was very dry for Chicago. By October, only six inches of rain had fallen. The city was a match stick waiting to be lit. In the residential quarter, homes were built of wood and most had an adjoining barn. Properties were separated by wooden fences. Unfinished wooden sidewalks ran in parallel paths down each street. In the business section, things were even worse. Factories of lumber, fabrics, and other highly flammable materials lined every block. The lack of rain and the everyday use of kerosene lanterns made fire a constant threat.

On the night of October 7, the worst fire in the history of Chicago began in Mrs. O'Leary's barn. The story says that the O'Leary's cow, impatient to be milked, kicked over a kerosene lamp. Quite possibly this is true because the fire did begin in the barn. However, what began as a routine barn fire quickly grew to astronomical proportions.

This 14k gold pocket watch is engraved with a picture of a lighthouse. It was found in the summer of 1989 by Tim Brown.

It's not uncommon to find an antique crockery or stoneware jug that is completely intact.

Fanned by 60-mile-an-hour winds, the fire spread throughout the west side of Chicago. Firefighters and civilians fought fiercely but could not contain it. Pieces of roofing, sparks, and smoldering debris were blown across the river igniting the south and north sides. Thousands of people watched as their homes or businesses burned to the ground in front of their eyes. The three-day fire devastated the city. Almost 100,000 people were made homeless. Seventy miles of street and over 17,000 buildings were completely destroyed. Chicago was declared a disaster area.

Reconstruction of the city began immediately. However, before new buildings could be constructed, the debris from the fire needed to be cleared away. Clean-up crews worked for months. The debris was loaded onto barges and dumped into Lake Michigan, creating a fantastic dive site.

Divers who enjoy finding artifacts should visit this site. Pottery, tools, bricks, and bottles abound in this area. Divers claim it's impossible to not find a souvenir worth keeping, and recovering these artifacts is not considered vandalization.

Wings of the Wind

Typical Depth: 45 feet
Typical Current: Variable: slight to mild
Expertise Required: Novice/intermediate
Access: Boat

The *Wings of the Wind* was the victim of a common occurrence on the lakes in the 1860s, a collision. Before the use of radar, ships were strictly limited to whistle signals and lookouts to prevent collisions. On the night of May 12, 1866, the *Wings'* lookout was at his post. It was an unusually dark night on the lake. Clouds blocked the moon's light and enveloped Lake Michigan in a blanket of blackness. All was quiet until 3 a.m., when the lookout cried out a warning. From out of the blackness another schooner suddenly appeared and bore down on them. The collision was unavoidable.

Crayfish, which look very much like saltwater lobster, can grow to over 6 inches in length.

A diver inspects the craftsmanship on this eighteenth-century steamer.

Hit amid ship, the *Wings* immediately started to take on water. The other schooner involved in the collision was the *H.P. Baldwin*. She survived unharmed. The captain of the *Wings* ordered lifeboats lowered, and all of the crew were successfully transferred to the *Baldwin*. Both crews watched as the *Wings of the Wind* sank until only her mastheads remained above water.

Later that same season, a salvage operation removed the *Wings'* cargo of coal. A bucket crane successfully removed the coal; however, in the process, the stern of the ship was severely damaged.

Today, the *Wings'* hull lies in 45 feet of water. Only the ribs of the stern section are left; however, the bow is completely intact. Her windlass is on deck and the front railing still stands.

5

Lake Huron

Sunday, November 9, 1913, dawned bright, with a light westerly wind and calm seas in lower Lake Huron. The upper end of the lake was a bit rough, but certainly nothing that the mighty lake freighters couldn't handle. Or so thought the captains of eight of the ships that entered the lake that day. Their ships might have survived a single weather system, but the storm that erupted over Lake Huron was caused by the collision of three fronts. One system approached from the north carrying freezing temperatures and blinding snow. The second system approached from the west bringing gale-force winds and more snow. These two systems merged into one gigantic force as they moved over the Great Lakes. But the worst was yet to come. A third system approached from the south, and with it came hurricane-force winds. When these two monstrous forces collided, they created the most ferocious storm the Great Lakes have ever experienced.

Colliding directly over Lake Huron, the two equally powerful storms deadlocked for forty-eight raging hours. The storm ravaged the lake and all who were on her waters. For sixteen straight hours the winds blew at more than 60 miles an hour, whipping the seas into towering 35-foot monsters. These massive walls of water advanced with ungodly velocity and followed one another in quick succession. The ships caught in the lake received incredible punishment. Blizzard conditions prevailed on shore. Railways came to a stop. Telegraphs were shut down. Whole towns were completely cut off from the rest of the world as over two feet of snow paralyzed the shorelines.

For the ships caught on the lake, the situation was desperate. Several attempted to head back to the safety of port. But when they turned into the trough of the invincible waves, they didn't stand a chance. Swamped or overturned, they went to the bottom. Other ships were suspended between two immense mountains of water. Their heavily loaded mid-sections stretched momentarily unsupported, thirty feet above the water, then broke apart and sank to their watery graves. Still others were driven onto rocks and shoals along both shorelines. Their crews huddled in terror as wave after wave threatened to destroy their ships. In all, over twenty ships were lost or stranded. Eight of the largest, costliest, and proudest ships disappeared with all hands. This one storm-gale-hurricane took over

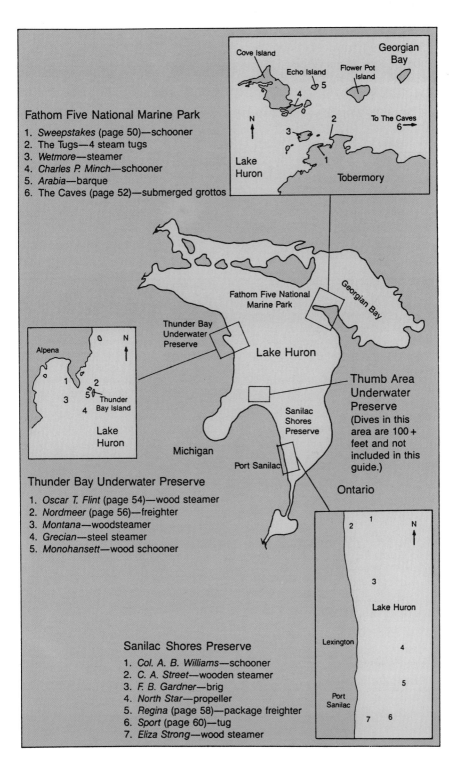

Fathom Five National Marine Park

1. *Sweepstakes* (page 50)—schooner
2. The Tugs—4 steam tugs
3. *Wetmore*—steamer
4. *Charles P. Minch*—schooner
5. *Arabia*—barque
6. The Caves (page 52)—submerged grottos

Cove Island

Echo Island

Flower Pot Island

Georgian Bay

N

To The Caves
6→

Lake Huron

Tobermory

Fathom Five National Marine Park

Georgian Bay

Lake Huron

Alpena

N

Thunder Bay Island

Lake Huron

Thunder Bay Underwater Preserve

Thumb Area Underwater Preserve
(Dives in this area are 100+ feet and not included in this guide.)

Sanilac Shores Preserve

Michigan

Port Sanilac

Ontario

Thunder Bay Underwater Preserve

1. *Oscar T. Flint* (page 54)—wood steamer
2. *Nordmeer* (page 56)—freighter
3. *Montana*—woodsteamer
4. *Grecian*—steel steamer
5. *Monohansett*—wood schooner

Lake Huron

Lexington

Port Sanilac

N

Sanilac Shores Preserve

1. *Col. A. B. Williams*—schooner
2. *C. A. Street*—wooden steamer
3. *F. B. Gardner*—brig
4. *North Star*—propeller
5. *Regina* (page 58)—package freighter
6. *Sport* (page 60)—tug
7. *Eliza Strong*—wood steamer

235 men and women to their graves. It was the most devastating storm in the history of the Great Lakes.

Lake Huron, the second largest of the Great Lakes, has more ships pass through its waters than Lake Superior and Lake Michigan combined. This is surprising because Lake Huron has no major cities of destination on its shores. For this reason, it has aptly been nicknamed the "Expressway" lake.

Georgian Bay, which bulges out of the northeastern corner of Lake Huron, is nearly as large as Lake Erie and was considered an additional Great Lake by early explorers. The entrance to the bay is guarded by the large island of Manitoulin and thousands of smaller islands. Manitoulin is the largest island in the Great Lakes. The passage between the southern tip of Manitoulin Island and the tip of the Bruce Peninsula is full of hidden, shallow reefs. Hundreds of ships have been lost on these shoals over the decades.

Today, the shipwrecks of Georgian Bay are protected by the Canadian National Parks System. The city of Tobermory, at the tip of the Bruce Peninsula, is a leading resort area for divers. The crystal clear waters of the bay are rivaled only by those of Lake Superior.

The Straits of Mackinaw, at the top of Lake Huron's west shore, also offer some fabulous diving. The straits connect two of the greatest bodies of water in the world, Lake Michigan and Lake Huron. This narrow passageway can be a dangerous area when the two mighty bodies of water come together in a storm. Nine intact shipwrecks litter the bottom here. The straits were designated in 1983 as one of Michigan's underwater preserves.

Further south, down Michigan's east coast, is the Great Lake's first underwater preserve: Thunder Bay. This area reportedly has the highest concentration of shipwrecks in all the lakes. It is aptly named "Shipwreck Alley." Thunder Bay contains wrecks dating from as far back as the mid-1800s to modern-day freighters.

Two underwater preserves have been established in lower Lake Huron: the Thumb Area Bottomland Preserve and Sanilac Shores Underwater Preserve. These preserves contain numerous virgin wrecks for the novice and the experienced diver to explore. Situated in lower Lake Huron, they are easily accessible to divers from many large metropolitan areas such as Detroit, Lansing, Toronto, Windsor, and Toledo.

The eastern coastline of Lake Huron is owned by the Canadian Province of Ontario. Because of the absence of natural harbors on this coast, Great Lakes shipping virtually passed this area by. Supplies were dropped off in Georgian Bay or at the port of Sarnia, Ontario, at the southern end of Lake Huron. For this reason, shipwrecks were less frequent here than in other parts of the lake.

The Fort Gratiot lighthouse at the base of Lake Huron guides ships to the safety of the St. Clair River. ▶

Sweepstakes

Typical Depth:	0 - 20 feet
Typical Current:	None
Expertise Required:	Novice
Access:	Boat or Shore, Fathom Five National Marine Park

The *Sweepstakes* is one of the most frequented dive sites in all the lakes. She was a wooden schooner built in Burlington, Ontario, in 1867. In August of 1885, she floundered off Cove Island in Georgian Bay. In

The temperature of the crystal clear waters surrounding the Sweepstakes *reaches the upper 60s during the summer.*

The Sweepstakes, *which is in less than 20 feet of water, can be enjoyed by snorkelers as well as divers.*

September 1885, salvagers towed her to the shallow waters of Big Tub Harbor. However, before they could complete their salvage operation she sank to the bottom.

Today, the *Sweepstakes* rests in approximately 20 feet of water, which makes it a perfect dive site for beginners and snorkelers. The wreck is fairly intact due mostly to the efforts of the Ontario Underwater Council (O.U.C.). Volunteers of the O.U.C. logged hundreds of hours of bottom time repairing the ice damage the hull suffered over the years. They reinforced the hull and decking with cables, oil drums, and bolts. Because of their restoration efforts, the *Sweepstakes* remains a unique underwater attraction for divers and snorkelers from all over Canada and the United States.

Divers can reach the *Sweepstakes* from shore; however, they should be prepared for a long swim. The wreck is about 200 yards from Big Tub Harbor Resort. Glass-bottomed boats regularly pass over the wreck, and park authorities suggest divers move to one side to allow the boats to pass.

The Caves

Typical Depth:	0 - 60 feet
Typical Current:	Slight
Expertise Required:	Novice
Access:	Boat, Fathom Five National Marine Park

Just around the bend from the quaint little village of Tobermory lies a series of underwater grottos locally known as "The Caves." These grottos were formed when the water level of Lake Huron was much lower. At that time, wave after wave smashed and battered the rock face. For thousands of years the waves eroded the Dolomite Cliffs, shaping and molding them like a potter with clay. Over centuries, the water level rose and the waves continued their never-ending sculpting higher up the wall.

Today, the entrance to the grotto lies in 20 feet of water. Entering here, divers swim through a 10 by 15-foot passageway to a large underwater room. Looking up, they can see sunlight beaming down from the surface. Following the layered shelf-like walls up to the surface, divers find themselves in a large open-air grotto.

It is possible to walk to the caves from the road. This makes a beautiful hike for swimmers or snorkelers. However, the winding two-mile trail (one way) is not recommended for divers carrying full scuba gear. Several dive charters run out every hour.

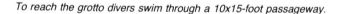

To reach the grotto divers swim through a 10x15-foot passageway.

The unique geological formations of the Niagara Escarpment provide fantastic photographic opportunities.

The charter boats in Tobermory can tie up to the rock cliffs. Divers only have to jump overboard and they are at the grotto entrance.

Oscar T. Flint

Typical Depth :	33 feet
Typical Current :	Moderate
Expertise Required :	Novice
Access :	Boat, Thunder Bay Underwater Preserve

Captain John Sinclair was sleeping peacefully in his cabin on the night of November 25, 1909, when he was awakened by the smell of smoke. He rushed from his cabin to find the entire bow of his ship in flames.

Stacks of steel pipe sit peacefully on the Flint's *deck, apparently undisturbed by the sinking.*

Here, a diver holds up a steel grate that was found on the stern of the Flint.

Captain Sinclair ordered the crew to lower the stern lifeboats and abandon ship. There was nothing they could do to save the *Oscar T. Flint*. The fire had already been spotted from shore, and before long the Thunder Bay Island lifesaving crew arrived to tow the *Flint*'s crew into town.

The *Flint* was a 240-foot wooden steamer that carried bulk cargos. She was upbound through Lake Huron with a load of limestone intended for Duluth and towed the barge *Redington*, which was also loaded with limestone. On Wednesday, November 24, the day before the fatal fire, the *Flint* pulled into Thunder Bay to do some minor engine repairs. At this time, the captain and crew had no idea that in less than twenty-four hours the *Flint* would burn to her waterline and sink.

The wrecked steamer now rests in 35 feet of water. The lake's bottom is littered with her scattered debris, although most of the hull and cargo of limestone is still intact. The boilers exploded as she went down showering the area with twisted metal. This is an excellent wreck for novice divers. The shallow depth allows plenty of time to investigate the boiler ruins, the hull, and the cargo, while still allowing time to enjoy the abundant marine life.

Nordmeer

Typical Depth :	0 - 40 feet
Typical Current :	Variable: slight to moderate
Expertise Required :	Novice/intermediate
Access :	Boat, Thunder Bay Underwater Preserve

The *Nordmeer* is one of the more recent wrecks on Lake Huron. It grounded on the night of November 19, 1966. Typically, a ship that goes down in November is lost because of a fierce northeastern gale. But that was not the case with the *Nordmeer*. Her destruction was caused by plain old human error.

The *Nordmeer* was upbound with a load of steel coils intended for the port of Chicago. It was a calm night and the crew did not anticipate any problems. However, without realizing his mistake, the first mate miscalculated the ship's course. He steered the ship directly onto Thunder Bay Shoal. The bottom of the 470-foot "salty" was ripped open in an instant. Lake Huron's waters poured into the ship's holds. The *Nordmeer* settled to the bottom with only seven feet of freeboard remaining above water.

The Nordmeer's *superstructure, which collapsed into the water in the summer of 1990, increases the fish habitat and interest of this dive. (Photo by Linda Bedell.)*

A diver examines some of the ship's tools that sit on the deck of the Flint in Thunder Bay Underwater Preserve.

All but eight of the crew were evacuated by the *Samuel Mathers*, an ore carrier that happened to be passing by. The captain and seven of the crew chose to remain behind to begin salvage operations. However, they didn't stay long because a November gale soon blew in. The captain put out another emergency call for help. On November 28, three days after grounding, he and the seven remaining crew members were rescued by the Coast Guard.

The *Nordmeer* is an excellent wreck for any level of diver. Its engine room lies in 30 to 40 feet of water. Snorkelers as well as divers can experience the magnitude of this huge saltwater freighter. Divers will enjoy swimming along the companionways and exploring the gigantic diesel engines that drove the ship to her grave. The schools of bass and perch that congregate around the wreck make this an underwater photographer's dream come true.

Regina

Typical Depth :	60 - 80 feet
Typical Current :	Variable: slight to moderate
Expertise Required :	Advanced
Access :	Boat, Sanilac Shores Underwater Preserve

On November 9, 1913, Captain McConkey steered the 249-foot steamer *Regina* onto Lake Huron. Like many other ship captains on the lake that day, he ignored the severe storm warnings being forecasted by the National Weather Service. It was November and some bad weather was to be expected. Unfortunately, this was no ordinary fall "blow." Within hours, Lake Huron became a raging beast. The tiny *Regina* did her best to fight the towering 30-foot waves and hurricane-force winds. For several hours,

The Regina's bell has been removed and is now traveling between Michigan's historical museums. (Photo by Wayne Brusate.)

The Regina was carrying cases of champagne and scotch when she went down. Most of the cargo has been salvaged. (Photo by Wayne Brusate.)

she struggled northward up the lake, until Captain McConkey finally made the decision to head back for the safety of the St. Clair River.

But Lake Huron had other plans for the *Regina* that day. When the bow turned parallel to the seas, the ship was suddenly caught in the trough of the gigantic waves. With the winds blowing from the NNW, and the seas running from the NNE, the *Regina* was trapped. Each wave smashed into her side, covering her decks with ice and possibly flooding her holds. In a desperate attempt to bring the ship around, Captain McConkey dropped the starboard anchor and put the rudder hard to starboard. But it was no use. The small 650-horse power engine was no match for the angry sea. Realizing the ship was doomed, McConkey gave the order to abandon ship. One lifeboat was successfully launched; however, the three crew members aboard succumbed to the freezing winds and snow before being washed ashore the next day. The remaining crew died that night in Lake Huron's freezing waters.

Today, the *Regina* lies upside down in 80 feet of water. Most of her original cargo of champagne, scotch, horseshoes, and spoons, and the ship's bell, chadburn, and compass have been salvaged. Most of these treasures are on display in various museums throughout Michigan. Divers visiting the wreck will find her name in brass letters on both the bow and stern. Her rudder, propeller, brass portholes and anchors, and one whistle are still intact and waiting for divers to enjoy.

Sport

Typical Depth:	50 feet
Typical Current:	None
Expertise Required:	Novice
Access:	Boat, Sanilac Shores Underwater Preserve

The *Sport* was a small harbor tug that spent most of its career on the St. Clair River and lower Lake Huron. Its duties included towing schooners through the rapids and into the lake, assisting barges and, for a time, carrying fishing charters. At first glance, the *Sport* appears to be just another small tug, but she isn't. The *Sport* was designed and built by Captain E. Ward. Captain Ward was a leader in the development of the steel and iron industries. At his Wyandotte steel mill, Ward used pieces of experimental steel to create the hull of the *Sport*, which is considered the first commercial steel vessel to ply the Great Lakes.

Quite by chance, the *Sport* played a major role in the storm of 1913. She was stationed in Port Huron when this mighty storm hit the area. In

The Sport's *superstructure is gone, but the ship's wheel is still on the wreck. (Photo by Wayne Brusate.)*

The Sport's bell was stolen by divers shortly after it was discovered. The Sport is just outside the Sanilac Shores Underwater Preserve. (Photo by Wayne Brusate.)

the aftermath of the storm, she was called upon to take local and marine officials and members of the press out to investigate a "mystery ship." This ship had been seen floating upside down at the surface. For several days there was much speculation as to which ship it was. Finally, a commercial diver, working from the *Sport*, identified the ship as the *Charles S. Price*.

The *Sport* was heading north towards Harbor Beach on Lake Huron's west shore on December 13, 1920, when a gale blew in from the southeast. The tug was overcome by the waves and went down. All of the crew, including the captain, managed to escape unharmed. Today, the *Sport* rests in 50 feet of water. This is a perfect site for divers new to wreck diving. The *Sport* sits upright on her sturdy steel hull. Although her bell was intact when she was found, it has since been stolen. However, divers will find her propeller, ship's wheel, one of her three whistles, and miscellaneous tools scattered over the bottom.

6

Lake Erie

Commander Oliver Perry was getting impatient. For three days he had been waiting for the British Naval Fleet to leave the safety of the Detroit River and enter the open waters of Lake Erie. Once the British entered the lake, Perry intended to draw them into a battle.

It was September 1813. The Americans had been at war with the British for over a year. Although the Americans had started the war, they weren't faring well. The major forts at Mackinaw, Detroit and Niagara had fallen to the British. The Americans desperately needed a victory. Perry felt sure he could gain that victory and secure the Great Lakes for the United States.

Finally, on September 10, the alarm was sounded; the British were entering the lake. Perry ordered his fleet of nine vessels out of Put-in-Bay. The British fleet of six vessels, under the command of Commander Barclay, advanced. The British ships had more long-range guns than did Perry's fleet. But Perry wasn't concerned. He planned to engage Barclay's fleet at close quarters, where his guns would do far more damage than Barclay's.

Thus the battle began. Barclay's ships immediately began firing their long-range guns. Though Perry's fleet received numerous blows, they were still able to close within firing range. Smoke and the smell of blood filled the air. The sound of splintering wood drifted across Lake Erie as masts and hulls were destroyed.

Commander Perry's ship was getting the worst of the firing. No less than 34 guns were bombarding his flagship, the *Lawrence*. Before long the ship was drifting helplessly, her sails and shrouds in shreds. Perry was desperate. Most of his crew was wounded or dead, and his ship was nearly destroyed. But he was not willing to surrender. He decided to abandon the *Lawrence* and assume command of the *Niagara*, the second largest ship of his fleet. She had hung back during most of the battle and hadn't received much damage. Perry climbed aboard a yawl with five of his remaining crew and headed for the *Niagara*. Enemy fire

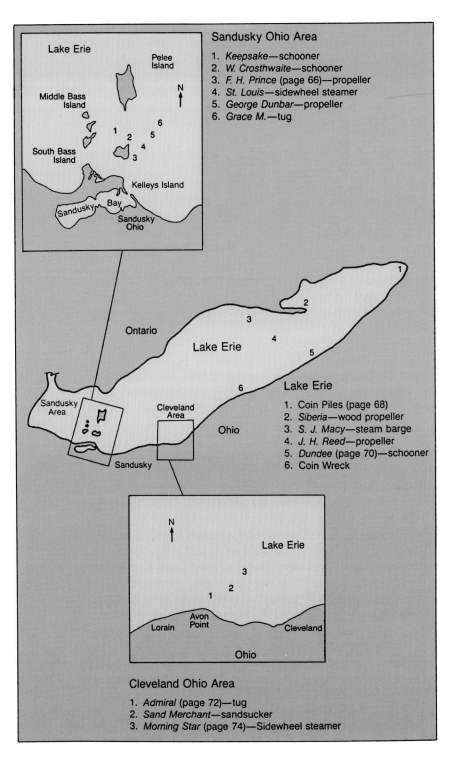

Sandusky Ohio Area

1. *Keepsake*—schooner
2. *W. Crosthwaite*—schooner
3. *F. H. Prince* (page 66)—propeller
4. *St. Louis*—sidewheel steamer
5. *George Dunbar*—propeller
6. *Grace M.*—tug

Lake Erie

1. Coin Piles (page 68)
2. *Siberia*—wood propeller
3. *S. J. Macy*—steam barge
4. *J. H. Reed*—propeller
5. *Dundee* (page 70)—schooner
6. Coin Wreck

Cleveland Ohio Area

1. *Admiral* (page 72)—tug
2. *Sand Merchant*—sandsucker
3. *Morning Star* (page 74)—Sidewheel steamer

63

showered the small row boat. Perry was undaunted. He stood proudly in the back of the boat, his war flag around his shoulders.

Once aboard the *Niagara*, Perry renewed his assault on the British. Barclay's fleet was suffering badly also. Most of his ships were severely damaged and his flagship drifted helpless. This new burst of energy and power by the Americans prevailed. Just fifteen minutes after Perry boarded the *Niagara*, the British surrendered. The Americans won. They had proven their superiority on the water and gained control over the Great Lakes. The only major naval battle ever fought on the Great Lakes was won by the Americans.

Lake Erie is the shallowest, oldest, busiest, and fiercest of the lakes. Because of its unpredictable nature, the lake was named "the cat" by the Indians who inhabited its shores. Erie's shallow depth, which averages 58 feet, can be turned into a raging beast within minutes. Storms blowing out of the west have been known to raise the water level at the eastern end of the lake by 13 feet. Mariners have greater respect for a storm on Lake Erie than on mighty Lake Superior. Today, hundreds of ships litter the bottom. Erie has the highest concentration of shipwrecks in the Great Lakes.

Lake Erie has been called the "dead lake" because of its pollution level during the 1960s and 70s. But efforts of environmentalists and stricter governmental regulations have restored the lake. Its waters are no longer dirty and gray. Visibility during the summer months commonly ranges from 20 to 30 feet. These factors combined with warm water temperatures (low 70s) and shallow depth make Lake Erie one of the best diving destinations in the Great Lakes.

Dive charters operate along the entire coast of Lake Erie. Buffalo, on the eastern end of the lake, is a large metropolitan area with numerous full-service dive shops. Cleveland, on the southern shore, offers some of the best wreck diving in the lake and an experienced dive-charter service. Sandusky Bay, at the western end of the lake, is the site of the battle of 1813. There are no regular diving charters in this area. However, most of the local dive shops will be happy to provide dive-site locations to divers with their own boats. The diving on Lake Erie's northern shore is as varied as the rest of the lake. Many ships were stranded on Point Pelee and Long Point, which protrude from Canada's southernmost coast. Diving charters can be arranged through several Ontario dive shops.

Two divers watch as a "laker" works its way down Lake Erie. ▶

F.H. Prince

Typical Depth:	3 - 15 feet
Typical Current:	Slight
Expertise Required:	Novice
Access:	Boat

How the *F.H. Prince* came to be resting on the east shore of Kelly's Inland is not known. She was a 245-foot wooden steamer built in the 1880s. Sometime during 1911, she caught fire and burned to her waterline. Whether the captain tried to beach her or whether she ran aground after being abandoned is a question for marine researchers to answer.

The shallow depth of this wreck makes it ideal for the novice diver. Most of the engine parts are still in place on the stern. The boiler lies only three feet below the surface. Keep this in mind when looking for this dive site, so your boat doesn't end up lying next to the *Prince*. The wreck isn't marked with a buoy. The hull stretches almost her full 245 feet. Many artifacts, from ceramic plates to steel spikes, are scattered in this area. Although this is not a protected area, divers should remember that other divers would enjoy seeing the artifacts.

The zebra mussel invasion has had a positive affect on Lake Erie's visibility. Since the invasion, the lake's average year round visibility has improved to 15-20 feet.

Lake Erie's warm, shallow waters are perfect for the growth of freshwater sponge and algae, as shown here on the Prince.

A large school of carp lives in the hull. Introduced in the 1880s by the United States Fish Commission, the carp were intended to be a food fish, however they never matched their popularity in Europe. These rather strange-looking fish can reach lengths of up to 2½ feet. With the magnification underwater, they seem to appear twice that size, and often startle divers who aren't accustomed to seeing such large fish in freshwater.

The bow of the *Prince* is separated from the rest of the wreck. Originally, it could be found about 50 feet to the west. However, in the last few years, it has been broken up by ice and wave action. Throughout most of the year, the wreck is covered with green and white freshwater sponge and several colorful algae. These marine organisms give the diver the feeling of reef diving. This, combined with an average visibility of 20 feet in the summer, make the *Prince* an inviting dive site.

67

Coin Piles

Typical Depth:	12 - 40 feet
Typical Current:	Slight to moderate
Expertise Required:	Novice/intermediate
Access:	Shore/boat

Two separate locations in Lake Erie are known as the "Coin Piles." One is located just north of Fairport Harbor on the south shore. The other is near Buffalo's harbor at the eastern end of the lake. Both of these sites contain the scattered remains of wooden sailing ships, although neither ship has been positively identified. In each area, coins that predate 1880 are regularly found.

Coin diving can be one of the most rewarding experiences for a diver or one of the worst. Every diver at one time or another has dreamed of finding the "mother lode." But, as most divers discover, searching for coins is a slow, painstaking process.

Most divers use a fanning technique. They begin in an area known to contain coins. Then, settling themselves onto the bottom, they gently sweep their hand back and forth two or three times. They then wait for the silt to clear and examine the area for any uncovered coins. If none appear, the gradual sweeping process continues until the diver reaches the clay or hard rock bottom. Many divers choose to wear dry suits when diving for coins, even in the summer, because this technique doesn't involve much diver movement.

Local dive shops can give divers specific instructions on how to reach the sites. Although both can be reached from shore, the Fairport site is a long swim, over ½ mile each way. Because both sites are near busy harbors, divers should be extremely cautious of boat traffic.

Half dollars, dimes, and one-cent pieces all from the late 1800s are frequently found at these sites. ▶

Dundee

Typical Depth:	50 - 80 feet
Typical Current:	Slight
Expertise Required:	Intermediate
Access:	Boat

On the night of September 11, 1900, Lake Erie was earning its reputation for ferocity. The small lake was a churning inferno. The seas were tremendous. The winds howled. The three-mast schooner *Dundee* was struggling across the lake. She was headed ultimately for Lake Superior with a load of iron ore.

The *Dundee* was in serious trouble by the time darkness settled over the lake. The high winds ripped her sails and each wave threatened to overturn her. Captain Singhas was particularly troubled, for several women were aboard ship, including his wife. As the ship began to go down, Captain Singhas lashed two women to a spar. His efforts were successful. These women, along with most of the crew who clung desperately to floating pieces of debris, drifted into shore and were saved. The only casualty was the female cook.

The *Dundee* is a fine example of a wooden schooner. Her hull is completely intact, except for her masts that were salvaged possibly for use on another ship. Divers will find many artifacts still in place, including the boom cradle, anchor housing and anchor chains. All of her holds are open and can be easily swum through. On the cross beam of the foremost hold, divers will find a set of numbers carved into the wood. These are the serial numbers that were used to positively identify the ship.

The Dundee*'s anchor chains flow out of the housings, then disappear off into the distance. (Photo by Russ MacNeal.)* ▶

Admiral

Typical Depth:	60 feet
Typical Current:	Slight
Expertise Required:	Intermediate
Access:	Boat

The *Admiral* was a 100-foot steel tug. She was built in 1922 and spent most of her life working out of Cleveland's harbor. On December 2, 1942, she was towing the barge *Clevco* into Cleveland. Lake Erie was in a foul mood that day. The seas were rough and the towline between the tug and barge jerked and strained. Suddenly, the *Clevco* was caught by a wave and was driven out to the side of the *Admiral*. The towline, which was connected close to the center of the *Admiral*, jerked the tug over onto her side. The crew aboard the *Clevco* struggled to cut the line. They succeeded in saving themselves but not the tug. The *Admiral* went down along with her crew of fourteen.

The Admiral's *air vent is almost large enough to hold a diver. (Photo by Russ MacNeal.)*

Lake Erie's visibility is often so good divers can see the entire length of the Admiral's deck. (Photo by Russ MacNeal.)

The *Admiral* now sits upright in 60 feet of water. The sand bottom is almost flush with the stern deck, completely covering the propeller. Cleats and miscellaneous pieces of working equipment are on the stern decking, and the towing harness is still standing.

The superstructure on the bow is completely intact. The pilot house and captain's quarters can be easily entered and investigated. Her anchor chains stretch out into the sand bottom; however, the anchors are not visible. Her smoke stack can also be seen lying on the bottom. Local divers worked over the last few years to remove the remains of the unfortunate crew members. All of the bones have been ceremoniously reburied a short distance from the wreck.

Morning Star

Typical Depth:	45 - 70 feet
Typical Current:	Slight
Expertise Required:	Intermediate
Access:	Boat

It was early 1868, and the side-paddle-wheel steamer *Morning Star* was headed out of Cleveland bound for Detroit. She was carrying 44 first-class passengers and an assorted cargo, including iron, nails, glass, cheese, and oil. The night was black, the seas were rough, and visibility was limited.

The schooner *Courtlandt* was on the same course as the *Morning Star*. While running under full sail, one of the *Courtlandt*'s crew members took down the running lights to clean them. Thus, the schooner became invisible to the approaching *Morning Star*. Just as the sailor aboard the *Courtlandt* replaced the lantern, the *Morning Star* rammed her broadside. In the confused seas, the schooner swung around and smashed into the *Morning Star*'s side-wheel. The churning paddles destroyed the side of the schooner. Finally breaking free of each other, both ships slowly sank to their watery graves.

Today, the *Morning Star* seems to belie her violent end. She sits upright in 70 feet of water and is almost completely intact. Her bow and the side-paddle-wheel that hit the *Courtlandt* are both destroyed. However, the remaining paddle is intact. The walking arm that turned both paddles is also intact and is surrounded with its decorative latch work. Divers can also find pieces of marble and brass fixtures from the first-class staterooms. Although this wreck is not in a designated preserve, divers should keep in mind that other divers would enjoy seeing these artifacts.

Most of Lake Erie's bottomland, including wrecks, is covered with zebra mussels, which were brought over from Europe in the bilges of freighters.

7

Lake Ontario

It was early evening and the *Hamilton* and *Scrouge* were becalmed. In fact, all the schooners in this part of Lake Ontario were listless. There hadn't been any wind for days. The lake's surface was smooth as glass and the once-powerful sailing ships drifted aimlessly.

Aboard the two schooners, the crews ate their evening meals, grumbled about the weather, then strolled to their sleeping quarters. The men weren't accustomed to inactivity. They were soldiers. The *Hamilton* and *Scrouge* were armed naval vessels under orders to patrol the western end of Lake Ontario for the Americans. The month was August, the year was 1813, and America was at war with the British. The soldiers were ready to fight, if mother nature would only make the winds pick up.

And pick up they did. A violent squall crossed the lake. Thick black clouds blocked out the moonlight. Then wind began to blow across the lake with such fury it turned the ships over on their sides. Blinding flashes and ear-splitting explosions filled the sky as the thunder and lightning began. Solid sheets of rain poured from the angry sky. The unwary *Hamilton* and *Scrouge* were immediately overcome.

The schooners had not been built for combat. They had been converted the year before to carry from eight to ten small cannons and one full-size cannon. This heavy artillery made the ships dangerously top heavy. When the squall hit, both schooners turned over onto their sides. With the weight of the cannons on deck, the ships instantly started to take on water and sink to their watery grave.

The crew members had only about four minutes' warning before the ships were lost. Most of the soldiers below decks never had a chance to escape. Many of the soldiers on deck were pinned by crates of ammunition and rigging. Their screams were drowned out by the howling winds and deafening roar of thunder. Lightning bolts illuminated the ships as they slipped beneath the surface of the raging inland sea.

Of the 50 or so crew members on each ship, only 8 survived. The *Hamilton* and *Scrouge* were discovered in 1975 in about 300 feet of water. Both vessels rest upright and are completely intact. With masts

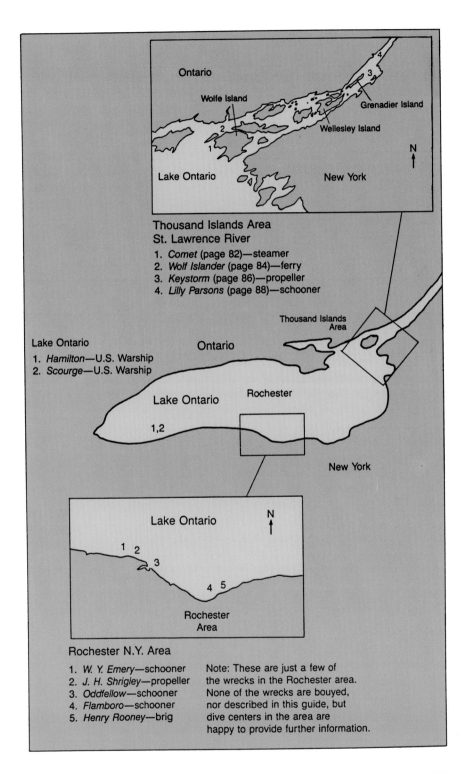

Ontario

Wolfe Island

Grenadier Island

Wellesley Island

Lake Ontario

New York

N

Thousand Islands Area
St. Lawrence River

1. *Comet* (page 82)—steamer
2. *Wolf Islander* (page 84)—ferry
3. *Keystorm* (page 86)—propeller
4. *Lilly Parsons* (page 88)—schooner

Thousand Islands
Area

Lake Ontario

1. *Hamilton*—U.S. Warship
2. *Scourge*—U.S. Warship

Ontario

Lake Ontario

Rochester

1,2

New York

Lake Ontario

N

Rochester
Area

Rochester N.Y. Area

1. *W. Y. Emery*—schooner
2. *J. H. Shrigley*—propeller
3. *Oddfellow*—schooner
4. *Flamboro*—schooner
5. *Henry Rooney*—brig

Note: These are just a few of
the wrecks in the Rochester area.
None of the wrecks are bouyed,
nor described in this guide, but
dive centers in the area are
happy to provide further information.

standing proud, cutglasses at the ready, and carronades in the gun ports, the ships still seem prepared to engage the enemy.

Lake Ontario is the smallest and last in the chain of the Great Lakes. Niagara Falls connects Lake Ontario with Lake Erie. Millions of gallons of water pass from Lake Erie, down the falls, and into Lake Ontario each hour. In fact, all the water in the Great Lakes eventually passes through Lake Ontario to the Atlantic Ocean.

Diving in Lake Ontario is centered at the eastern end of the lake. Most storms that pass through Lake Ontario travel from west to east. Ships caught in the lake are almost always carried to the eastern end of the lake where they either find a safe harbor or are wrecked on the numerous reefs and islands.

The entrance to the St. Lawrence River is also at the eastern end of Lake Ontario. The St. Lawrence is a vital link between the Great Lakes and the Atlantic Ocean. The area where the waters of Lake Ontario end and the waters of the St. Lawrence begin is called the Thousand Islands. This stretch of water is filled with hidden reefs and dotted with hundreds of small islands. It is one of the most treacherous areas to navigate in the Great Lakes system. Hundreds of ships have gone down here, creating an underwater paradise for wreck divers.

Visibility at the east end of Lake Ontario is normally 20 to 30 feet. The lake's temperatures reach the upper 60s in the summer, and most dives are under 100 feet. This is the ideal location for divers who want good wreck diving in warm, clear waters.

Rochester, New York, and Toronto, Ontario, are two of the largest cities on Lake Ontario's shore. Both areas have numerous wrecks within a short distance of their harbors. Unfortunately, no charter services are available in either area, nor are any of the sites buoyed. However, both cities have several full-service dive centers. These shops are happy to assist divers with information about dive sites in their area.

A good drysuit can make fall diving a fun and rewarding experience. Here, divers prepare to make a shore dive in the 1000 Islands area. ▶

Thousand Islands

Typical Depth:	0 - 60 feet
Typical Current:	Slight to moderate
Expertise Required:	Novice
Access:	Shore

Back in the "good old days," before plastic containers, almost everything was put into bottles, from milk and medication to ant poison. And, as was the habit in those days, once anything was emptied it was thrown into the water. This tradition has created superb bottle diving in the Great Lakes.

The entire Thousand Islands area of Lake Ontario is littered with old bottles, pottery, and artifacts. Because most of these islands have been occupied for hundreds of years, divers can make great discoveries almost anywhere. There are numerous reference books that can help divers to recognize older bottles. However, there are several markings a diver can check while still underwater. Any bottle that is embossed (has raised lettering) is more valuable than one that isn't. The length of the seam that runs up the side of the bottle can help determine its age. Generally, the higher up the neck the seam goes, the newer the bottle. For example, if the seam ends at the base of the neck the bottle was probably made before 1860. If the seam extends all the way up the neck and through the lip, the bottle was made after 1903.

Medicine bottles are fun to find and collect. They are usually embossed and could have contained just about anything, from Comstock Brothers Turkish Balm to Dr. Kilmer's Swamp Root.

The color of the glass is also something to watch for. Aqua is the natural color of glass and will usually signify an old bottle. But blue glass is the favorite color of most collectors. A blue bottle with embossing is one of the best finds a diver can make.

Bottles with round bottoms are also good finds. To keep the corks moist, the owner laid these bottles on their sides, therefore, there was no need for a flat bottom. Round-bottomed bottles were carried as ballast on sailing ships from Europe. These bottles could be easily stacked and they provided good stability for the ships.

Keep in mind that most bottles are only worth a few dollars to antique collectors. Their real value is to the diver who recovers them, cleans them up, and proudly displays them.

One era's trash is another era's treasure! Here two bottles tempt a diver closer. ▶

Comet

Typical Depth:	75 - 85 feet
Typical Current:	Moderate to strong
Expertise Required:	Advanced
Access:	Boat

The *Comet* was a wooden side-wheel steamboat built in 1860. She was 158 feet long, had double decks, and was painted a stately white. Because she was a passenger steamer, she was outfitted with several large saloons and plush private cabins. The ship was elegantly furnished and provided passengers with all the luxuries of a grand hotel.

Side-wheel steamboats carried thousands of passengers to their destinations in the 1800s, but not all trips were successful.

When the steam engine became practical in the late 1700s, ship builders around the lakes searched for ways to use it to make ships faster. Many different techniques were tried. One early design included a row of upright paddles on either side of the ship that dipped into the water like Indian canoe paddles. Another design used screw propellers. This design failed because of weak iron and insufficient steam pressure. Finally, in 1807, Robert Fulton designed the side-wheeler. He felt that two wheels, one on either side of the ship, would provide a good "bite" in the water. The side-wheelers proved successful. They were easily maneuverable and quite fast, averaging three miles an hour. Soon side-wheelers were seen steaming all across the Great Lakes.

Later versions of the side-wheelers, like the *Comet*, bore little resemblance to the first crude side-wheelers. For one thing, they were much faster; the *Comet* averaged 15 miles per hour. Even when propellers became practical in the 1840s, the paddle boats still had many advantages. They could maneuver better and started and stopped much more quickly. The paddles on either side offered more stability; therefore, the ships could be built higher, like layered cakes. An extra bonus of the side-wheeler was the romantic appearance their graceful rounded humps gave to the ship. The housings that covered the paddle wheels were decorated with pictures and fancy trim, and the ship's name was painted in large gold letters.

In 1869, the *Comet* came to the end of her career. Her engines were removed and placed aboard the new steamer *Corona*. She was then sold to Captain Cobb to be used as a barge. How she came to be resting on the bottom of Lake Ontario is not clear. It is possible that while in use as a barge, she was swamped or capsized and went down.

Regardless of how she got there, the *Comet* is a fascinating dive. Her side-paddle wheels are still intact and offer divers a unique look into an era long past. Her decking is mostly intact; however, divers should not consider penetrating. Because she had many cabins and saloons, it would be easy to get lost inside. Besides, the true beauty of this wreck is found in the overall view of the paddle wheels and outside decking.

Wolfe Islander

Typical Depth:	70 - 80 feet
Typical Current:	Moderate
Expertise Required:	Intermediate
Access:	Boat

The *Wolfe Islander* is unique because it has been purposely sunk for the enjoyment of divers. It was built in 1940 at Collingwood, Ontario. For several decades, it served as a car ferry between Kingston, Ontario, and Wolfe Island. By the late 1960s, it was replaced by a larger, more efficient ferry. Canada's ministry of transportation donated the ship to the Marine Museum at Kingston. The museum, in turn, donated the *Islander* to the Comet Foundation, which masterminded its sinking for the diving community.

Sculpins can be seen all across the Great Lakes. They are normally seen resting on bottom waiting for lunch to swim by.

The Wolfe Islander *is one of the few wrecks in the Great Lakes that was purposely sunk for divers' enjoyment.*

Volunteers from the Comet Foundation spent months working on the ship before it was sunk. All traces of gasoline and pollutants were removed. The decks were cleared and made as safe as possible for divers. And a stainless steel time capsule was mounted on the starboard rail (car deck level). The capsule, which is to be opened in fifty years, contains letters from politicians, cassette tapes of music, newspaper clippings, and personal letters from several members of the foundation.

Today, the wreck sits in 80 feet of water, although most of the superstructure is in 70 feet. Divers can easily swim through all three levels. This is a fairly safe wreck because there are very few places to penetrate. The *Wolfe Islander* is a great wreck for beginners; however, because of the depth, it is considered an intermediate dive.

Keystorm

Typical Depth:	20 - 110 feet
Typical Current:	Moderate to strong
Expertise Required:	Advanced
Access:	Boat

The *Keystorm* was a 250-foot steel freighter. She was built in 1910 in Canada; however, she was registered in London, England. On October 12, 1912, a dense fog covered eastern Lake Ontario. The two-year-old *Keystorm* was headed into the lake. While running under full steam, she struck Scow I Outer Shoal. All of her crew safely made it to shore before she settled to the bottom.

The *Keystorm* was one of the small, early freighters. She could carry 1,673 gross tons, which was impressive in those days. Today's super freighters can carry well over 15,000 tons. When the *Keystorm* went down, she was carrying a full load of coal, which was later salvaged.

The Keystorm's bow is in 15-20 feet of water; however, be careful of the strong current in this area.

Divers appear small compared to the large blades of a freighter's propeller.

The bow of the *Keystorm* rests in approximately 15 to 20 feet of water. The rest of the wreck slants down to 110 feet. She is perfectly intact and lies on her starboard side. Both her fore and aft superstructures are open and can be easily swum through. Although she was a small ship by today's standards, her empty, gaping holds are still overwhelming to a six-foot diver. Descending to the stern, divers find the *Keystorm*'s name printed in brass letters. The propeller or screw is also still in place.

The *Keystorm* is an advanced dive because of the strong current conditions in the area. The deck and superstructure are on the downstream side of the wreck, which means they are shielded from the strong currents. When diving from a private boat, make sure someone stays topside to watch for divers who might get pushed downstream and have trouble returning to the boat.

Lilly Parsons

Typical Depth:	50 - 60 feet
Typical Current:	Moderate to strong
Expertise Required:	Advanced
Access:	Boat

The *Parsons* succumbed to the same fate as many of the wooden-hulled ships. She was abandoned. Steel-hulled ships carried more cargo and traveled faster than the older sailing ships. These steel ships made the wooden boats obsolete. Many, like the *Parsons*, were left to rot and eventually sink.

Although she did not have a heroic end, the *Parsons* is an interesting dive. To reach the wreck, divers must first dock their boat on the south side of Sparrow Island. The island is located just south of Brockerville, Ontario, on the St. Lawrence River. Walking to the north side of Sparrow Island, divers find a large anchor on shore. The anchor chain leads from shore to the bow of the wreck in approximately 50 feet of water. At the end of the anchor chain, divers find a commemorative plaque nailed to the *Parsons'* bow. This plaque explains what type of ship she was, when she was launched, and how she was lost.

Because of the strong current on this wreck and the heavy boat traffic, divers should always enter and exit the water at the anchor chain.

Save Ontario Shipwrecks (S.O.S.)

Save Ontario Shipwrecks (S.O.S.) is a nonprofit organization that has been at the forefront of shipwreck preservation. Volunteer members of S.O.S. spent hours underwater surveying the *Parsons*. They set up a small artifact display case on the port side near the stern. Plates, glasses, bottles, and other artifacts can be held and inspected by visiting divers. S.O.S. has also attached a series of small tags throughout the ship. These tags identify objects and explain the ship's construction. Not only is this underwater museum informative and a great dive, but it also helps to remind divers of the importance of marine preservation.

This deadeye with an attached strap is another example of the type of rigging that was removed before the ship was abandoned. ▶

Appendix 1 — Recompression Chambers

DAN (Divers Alert Network) is a membership association that maintains a 24-hour emergency hotline. DAN's operators can provide advice on treatment, evacuation, and recompression chambers. Divers who need emergency services should call DAN's emergency number before trying specific area chambers because the status of these chambers changes frequently.

DAN: 919-684-8111

Thunder Bay, ONT.: 807-623-7451

Marquette, MI: 906-225-3560

Chicago, IL: 312-878-6000

Milwaukee, WI: 414-649-6577

Kalamazoo, MI: 616-341-7778

Tobermory, ONT.: 519-596-2305

Toledo, OH: 419-381-4172

Buffalo, NY: 716-887-4600

Toronto, ONT.: 416-595-4131 Day
416-595-3155 Night

Appendix 2 — Dive Shops and Charter Services

This list is included as a service to the reader. The author has made every effort to make this list complete at the time the book was printed. This list does not constitute an endorsement of these operators and dive shops. If operators/owners wish to be included in future reprints/editions, please contact Pisces Books, P.O. Box 2608, Houston, Texas 77252-2608.

LAKE SUPERIOR

Scuba Adventures, Inc.
1080 Roselawn Ave.
Roseville, MN 55113
612-487-3440
Isle Royale, North Shore

Grand Island Ventures
RR 1, Box 436
Mill Street
Munising, MI 49862
906-387-4477
Alger Underwater
Preserve, Munising

Superior Scuba
120 Ann St.
Sault Saint Marie,
MI 49783
906-632-1332
Whitefish Bay
Underwater Preserve

LAKE MICHIGAN

Marine Discoveries
8611 Gross Point Rd.
Skokie, IL 60077
708-673-4628
Chicago

Berry Scuba
6674 Northwest Hwy.
Chicago, IL 60631
312-763-1626
Chicago

Pirates Cove Diving, Inc.
1103 W. Oklahoma Ave.
Milwaukee, WI 53215
414-482-1430
Milwaukee

Silent World Divecenter Inc.
723 Virginia Ave.
Sheboygan, WI 53081
Sheboygan

Rec Diving
4224 N. Woodward Ave.
Royal Oak, MI 48072
800-999-0303
Straits of Mackinaw

Scuba North
13380 W. Bayshore Dr.
Traverse City, MI 49684
616-947-2520
Manitou Passage
Underwater Preserve

Rod's Reef
3134 W. Johnson Rd.
Ludington, MI 49431
616-843-8688
Southeastern Lake
Michigan

LAKE HURON

G & S Watersports Ltd.
Box 21
Tobermory, ONT.
NOH 2RD
519-596-2200
Georgian Bay

Rec Diving
4224 N. Woodward Ave.
Royal Oak, MI 48072
800-999-0303
Straits of Mackinaw

Thunder Bay Divers
160 E. Fletcher
Alpena, MI 49707
517-356-9336
Thunder Bay Underwater
Preserve

Macomb Dive
28869 Bunert
Warren, MI 48093
313-774-0640
Sanilac Shores
Underwater Preserve

LAKE ERIE

Underwater Enterprises
832 Lake Ave.
Elyria, OH 44035
216-323-9542
Southwestern Lake Erie

Outer Reef Dive Center
1 Main St.
Port Dover, ONT.
NOA 1NO
519-583-1050
Northern Lake Erie

Dip and Dive, Inc.
500 Niagara Falls Blvd.
Buffalo, NY 14223
716-837-DIVE
Eastern Lake Erie

LAKE ONTARIO

Aquatic Center of Rochester
2199 E. Henrietta Rd.
Rochester, NY 14623
716-334-1670
Eastern Lake Ontario

T.A.M. Dive
246 King St. East
Toronto, ONT.
416-861-1664
Toronto area

Index